The Bitter Berry
THE LIFE *of*
BYRON HERBERT REECE

By Bettie Sellers

D1447365

GEORGIA HUMANITIES COUNCIL
Southern Literature Series

Georgia Humanities Council
Atlanta, Georgia 30322

ISBN 0-8203-1522-2

The Georgia Humanities Council receives support through grants from the National Endowment for the Humanities. The views herein do not necessarily represent those of the Georgia Humanities Council and the National Endowment for the Humanities.

WITH VERY SPECIAL THANKS TO

Dr. Raymond Cook for his fine book
*Mountain Singer: The Life and Legacy
of Byron Herbert Reece*.

Contents

About This Publication

BYRON HERBERT REECE lived, farmed, and wrote in the hills and valleys of northern Georgia. His poetry draws its images from that region as it draws language and form from the English ballad tradition and the Bible.

The documentary video, "The Bitter Berry: The Life and Work of Byron Herbert Reece," invites viewers to see Reece's North Georgia landscape while they hear his poems. Scenes from his quiet life as a farmer and teacher and words from his own journal provide a sense of the man. The video has received a Red Ribbon Award from the American Film and Video Festival and an "Emmy" award for Best Overall Achievement, Cultural Affairs Program, from the Georgia Chapter, National Academy of Television Arts and Sciences, as well as other awards in recognition of its excellence.

"The Bitter Berry" video was written by Bettie Sellers, who co-produced it with Gary Moss and George deGolian. Gary Moss directed the production.

This publication will be particularly useful as a study guide to accompany the documentary. The video and the guide taken together form a unit in the series, "Southern Literature," developed by the Georgia Humanities Council with financial support from the National Endowment for the Humanities. The series is designed to make available to the general public the results of scholarly research on Georgia and the South in the fields of study known as the humanities. Among these fields are literature and language, philosophy and ethics, history, and archaeology, all of which are basic in school and college education. The contributions of specialists in the humanities and their writings are indispensable resources for interpreting our cultural heritage and reexamining our values.

This publication amplifies the description of Reece's life and work offered in the film, and looks at the poems discussed in the film as well as other examples of Reece's writings. A discussion leader may draw on this publication as a resource in preparing a program and may also make it available to participants. Viewers of the documentary who would like to extend their knowledge of Byron Herbert Reece will find the guide both useful and thought-provoking. The discussion questions provided are open-ended, and are intended to suggest ways of fostering exploration of the issues and of the poems, as well as examining the filmmaker's techniques. The discussion leader may select those questions of most interest to a particular group. Members of the group will undoubtedly bring their own knowledge, experience, and interests to the conversation.

The selection of additional poems includes many of those mentioned in either the documentary video or within the text of this publication. The suggestions for further reading will be of interest to those who would like to read Reece's work for themselves or to learn more about his life.

We hope that these materials will stimulate the development of program series by local libraries, historical societies, church and civic groups, and other organizations. Arrangements to borrow a copy of the documentary or to obtain copies of this guide may be made by contacting the Georgia Humanities Council, 1556 Clifton Road N.E., Emory University, Atlanta, Georgia 30322; telephone (404) 727-7500. Information is also available about other programs in this series, and about grant programs of the Georgia Humanities Council through which groups may seek support for educational programs.

Mary Drake McFeely
Series Editor

Introduction

EARLY IN 1945, the young North Georgia poet Byron Herbert Reece sent a six-line untitled poem to *The Progressive Farmer*. Published in their "Letters to the Editor" column, it sums up the life and writing of the man:

> These hills contain me as a field, a stone,
> Yet I contain them also: when I fare
> Beyond their borders and am all alone
> I need but think of them to see them there,
> Each hill, each hollow, each familiar place
> As clearly imaged as a loved one's face.

The hills and valleys that contain most of the life and death of the poet are located in northern Georgia near the North Carolina line. His birthplace was Choestoe, called by the Cherokee "The Land of Dancing Rabbits" and his place of death was Young Harris, in the Brasstown Valley that runs northward from Enotah Bald, the highest mountain in Georgia.

Reece was born on September 14, 1917 in an old log cabin by Wolf Creek, of a family that had lived in the area from the final years of the Cherokee occupation. Both paternal and maternal great-grandfathers had been among the earliest settlers in the region and were known to have had good relationships with the Indians who lived nearby. Byron (or "Hub" as he was called by family and friends) was the fourth living child of Juan and Emma Reece. Alwayne, the first-born, had died of meningitis at thirteen months. Eva Mae was born in 1911, Nina Kate in 1914, T.J. in 1915, Byron Herbert in 1917, and Jean in 1923. By 1921, the one-room cabin was crowded. Juan Reece moved his growing family a short distance down the creek to the house where Emma Reece had grown up. The site of the original cabin where Reece was born, a place called in Cherokee "The Place of the Morning Star," is now covered by the waters of Lake Vogel.

ONE *Early Years*

CHOESTOE, IN UNION COUNTY, Georgia, was an isolated spot during the years of Reece's youth. Roads were mostly dirt, neighbors miles away. Daily Bible readings supplied both entertainment and religious studies, and the boy who would be a poet trained his ear on the cadences of the Psalms in the King James Version. "He was always standing off somewhere, looking, observing. He was a deep boy," wrote a cousin, remembering young Reece's personality during their years at Choestoe Elementary School. Because of his reading ability, he was advanced from first grade to third. At home with *Pilgrim's Progress* and the King James Version of the Bible, he was bored with the popular "Baby Ray" primers and spent much time listening to the older students who shared the classroom.

Reece attended Union County High School in Blairsville, Georgia from September, 1931 to May, 1935. Here the voracious reader's talent for writing was recognized. His English teacher, the school principal, Dr. James M. Nicholson, remembered Byron as a high-school boy so shy that he left his original poems under his teacher's door. Two years after he left high school, in 1937, Reece burned all the poems he had written up to that time. But in June of the same year, his first poem to be published outside the local area appeared in *Kaleidograph*, a literary journal published at Georgia State College for Women in Milledgeville, Georgia.

On February 10, 1936, recommending Reece for admission to Young Harris College, some eighteen miles north in Towns County, Dr. Nicholson characterized Reece as having an "unusual mentality." "Few people understand him," his former teacher observed. "Cynical, truthful, dependable, determined. Has few contacts with folks, and *wants* but few. Except in mathematics, he is about the best pupil we have sent you. Widely read. Tastes are literary and artistic. Writes unusually good poetry and short stories, but is like Thoreau about his work. Knows he has ability, but doesn't give a straw whether you know it or not."

Reece attended Young Harris during the 1935-36 school year, dropped out to keep the family farm running, and returned during 1936-39. His brother T.J. had joined the Civilian Conservation Corps in 1937. His parents were both ill with tuberculosis. The eldest son still at home, he was needed frequently on the farm. The eighteen courses (primarily in English, History, and Education) he took at Young Harris during those two years constituted his academic training. The needs of his family and his lack of interest in French and Mathematics prevented him from graduating.

Nevertheless, he made a name for himself in college and in literary publications. In August of 1938, Professor W. Lufkin Dance, who sponsored the Quill

Club of student writers, wrote to one of the members: "A Reece boy who has already published poems in both *Harper's* and *Mercury* will be with us next year." In October, Philip Greear, a student who became a close friend of Reece, reported in the campus newspaper that since 1934, when Byron's first poem was published in a local newspaper, thirty-one of his poems had appeared in such journals as *Kaleidograph, Circle, Arcadian Life Magazine, Poetry World,* and in some nine annual anthologies of American and world poetry.

In the summer and fall of 1939, young Reece wrote a column, "Pegasus' Tracks," for the campus newspaper, *The Enotah Echoes.* He wrote in the December issue, "People who cannot appreciate poetry miss part of their heritage. It is a pity not to be able to see the poetry in life, and the life in poetry..." With the help of Professor Dance, the students of The Quill Club published three annual volumes of a literary review, *If Eyes Were Made For Seeing.* And, although Reece was not a student at the college for all of that time, of the 144 poems in these three volumes, thirty-one were his. It is possible that the poet had some impact on the publication of the review, since he had complained in his final "Pegasus' Tracks" column that sports and banquets were taking too much of both time and money. "I hope," he continued, "that in the future the students may have a literary quarterly in which to express their creative urge."

The poems Reece wrote during his brief college days display those themes which would continue to engage his interest throughout his writing career of some twenty more years. The poignant "Whose Eye is on the Sparrow," which first appeared in "Pegasus' Tracks," as well as several early poems later revised, were included in *Ballad of the Bones and Other Poems,* published in 1946. "Therefore the Mote" from *Bow Down in Jericho* is a variation of the following untitled piece from the column:

> Shadow to shadow
> O brown rabbit
> In the green hedge,
> The hound's habit's
> To hunt the edge.
>
> Therefore lie
> In the cool shade
> In the green center
> Of the alder glade.
>
> And where the leaves
> Are thick on the ground
> Dream of the race
> With the yelping hound.

That you and he –
And I – must run
Shadow to shadow
In the thin sun.

The close communion with the brown rabbit, the ever-threatening yelp of the hounds, the shadow of death hovering close by would echo in his poems through four major volumes, and in the large body of correspondence which he carried on with friends through the years.

Another column included a verse couched in the form of nursery rhyme, but filled again with this theme of death which would characterize so much of the mature poet's work:

NURSERY RHYME

Death is a baker,
Or so I have heard,
And life is the fowler
That catches the bird
That is baked in his pie.
The pie being done
Is set to cool
Away from the sun.
And true to the fable
We birdies must sing
To make it a dainty dish
Fit for the king.

In late 1939 Ralph McGill, the crusading editor of *The Atlanta Constitution*, visited the Young Harris College campus with Walter Rich, a new trustee. McGill had read a Reece poem in *Mercury* and asked about the Blairsville man who had written it. A teacher arranged to take McGill to the Working Gang House where Reece lived. There McGill met the young man and saw more of his poems. McGill remembered that "Byron, perhaps then more than later, had the looks of the young Lincoln. He was gaunt and so thin as to seem taller than he was." The friendship that began then lasted throughout Reece's lifetime.

TWO *The Farmer-Poet*

FROM THE TIME REECE left Young Harris College until 1945, he worked on the farm by day and wrote at night. During the years before 1941, he followed world events with increasing concern. After the bombing of Pearl Harbor, he went to Atlanta with the intention of joining the army. He had been deferred earlier because of family and farming responsibilities; this time his extreme thinness and the increasing incidence of tuberculosis in the family caused another deferment. In the many letters he wrote to former classmates overseas during the war, he frequently mentioned his feeling of guilt that he was not able to be with them. In an undated letter to Pratt Dixon, a young California poet with whom he carried on a correspondence of many years, he commented that he had been sawing wood all day, and continued:

> as I sat before the fire too tired to move I thought what a peaceful, what a virtuous world this would be if everybody had to tail a wood saw every day…. If people had enough work to do to keep them healthily occupied, then notions to blow up their neighbor would be considerably less likely to drive them down a blind alley to destruction.

During these years his poems continued to appear in poetry journals and magazines around the country. In 1942, he was featured in an anthology entitled *Three Lyric Poets*, published in Prairie City, Illinois, in an edition of 250 copies. In 1943, when he was supplementing his farm income by sometime teaching at Zion Elementary School in Union County, he was "discovered" by a noted Kentucky writer Jesse Stuart. Stuart wrote to Reece after reading the ballad, "Lest the Lonesome Bird," in *Prairie Schooner*. In the memorial issue of *The Georgia Review*, published after Reece's death in 1958, Stuart remembered:

> I had never heard of Byron Herbert Reece, but now I had heard of him and his name would be one, even if he did only this one poem, that would stick in my memory as long as I lived. He had written a poem that seemed to have written itself . . . a poem I wish I had written. It was one of his ideas that had always been with me, but he had discovered and clothed it in his simple language of understandable genius. Here was a poet.

The Kentucky poet and novelist asked for and received a sheaf of poems from the young man. He took them to his own publisher, E.P. Dutton, and in 1945, Dutton published Reece's first major volume, *The Ballad of the Bones and Other Poems*. The title poem is based on Ezekiel 37, in which God urges Ezekiel to "prophesy upon these bones." It was named the best poem of that year by the journal *American Poet*.

The mailman brought the first copies of *Ballad of the Bones* to the farm on September 17, 1945, Reece's twenty-eighth birthday. He was in the field mowing hay and only returned to the house long enough to show his father and mother the dedication, "For Juan and Emma." Celebration was in order, but the hay field would not wait.

After he returned to the field, a deadly copperhead snake struck as he passed on the mower, but the blades killed it. He saw this as a good sign. The snake appeared in a poem included in a later volume.

THE HAYING

To the fields at break of day
The mowers go to cut the hay.

Something is hiding in the green
Field that hates the iron machine.

It hisses so it wakes the hives
Of anger in the sickle's knives.

All day long these war, and make
Sounds like scissors and a snake.

Many reviews followed the publication of *Ballad of the Bones*. One stands out as typical and to the point: "Like a clean wind blown down from the Georgia hills," wrote the critic in *The Atlanta Journal*, "comes the discovery of Byron Herbert Reece, whose poetry falls as simple and natural as sunlight across the fields, upon the inner recesses of the mind." The response to the book was so good that E.P. Dutton had brought out a third printing by January, 1946.

Ballad of the Bones included nine ballads. Noting Reece's gift for this form, Sarah Henderson Hay, in the *Saturday Review of Literature*, commented that the poet was "so steeped in the great tradition of Biblical and Elizabethan literary form that its qualities and characteristics seem as natural to him as breathing." Ballads, like Bible verses, had been part of his upbringing. In an essay entitled "Songs My Mother Taught Me," Reece wrote: "My parents remember that forty years ago one of the commonest forms of social recreation was to congregate at the home of someone, preferably a person of good voice who knew a lot of songs, and sing away the Sunday afternoons." He remembered the pure, clear quality of his mother's voice as she sang "The Three Little Babes" as a lullaby for him and his siblings. He later learned that this ballad probably derived from the earlier "The Wife of Usher's Well," and was "probably a version native to Georgia. We are very nearly pure Anglo-Saxon stock here in the Georgia mountains, and a lot of English threads have come down in our heritage. Two or three touches are certainly native." He stated that it was customary for the mountain singer in this country to add touches characteristic of the hills and life of his own area. "The Jealous Lover" was a favorite with mountain singers, since "they prefer the strong emotional meat of tragedy to the light wine of comedy."

When Byron Reece was about fifteen, Professor James C. Camp was combing the valleys, listening to the old timers sing the ballad songs not yet written down. He cites "Bright Brasstown Valley" (a song about the valley adjacent to Choestoe) as a local version of "Red River Valley" and found other regional versions of older ballads, such as "Union County Jail," among the eighteen ballads still being sung in the area surrounding Reece's Choestoe Valley home. That old and new versions of the ballads were still being orally transmitted in the growing years of Byron Reece is well documented by Professor Camp's work.

"Ballad of the Bones," the title piece of the first book, is inspired by the language of Ezekiel in the King James Version of the Bible (for which Reece expressed a preference in an undated letter to Pratt Dixon) but the freshness of metaphor comes from the poet's observation of the Appalachian countryside he loved. The bones of the valley are "dry as grass in a drought" that might be observed in a mountain pasture in late summer, stones are "dark as soot," bones "dry as faggots" and "clean as a peg." The skeletons assembled are likened to a wood "when winter grieves in the branches bare of the shape of leaves."

"Lest the Lonesome Bird," the poem so admired by Jesse Stuart, also employs images from nature--ridges "curtained by the rain," a familiar sight in the foothills which surround Reece's home in Choestoe, and hills "green with the young leaf." This harsh story of murder and guilt reflects the old law of blood vengeance which still occasionally erupts from the valley. Sounds intensify the atmosphere: the kettle is whistling through the spout, and the tormented lover is likened to an angry cat. In this poem, as in "Ballad of the Rider" and in five ballads that appear in *Bow Down in Jericho* ("The Riddles," "The Fable in the Blood," "To Dance Go They," "Pretty Polly," and "The Heart in the Hand"), Reece shows his continued interest in the tradition theme of the jealous lover so popular with earlier ballad singers.

In "Ballad of the Weaver," a favorite which ultimately appeared in two versions, old Margot, whose lifetime of weaving has made many garments, from the "warm cloth that swaddled/the new-crying child" to robes for the bride and jeans for the groom, experiences loneliness and grief as she discovers that "whose lord is a rover/Her house keeps alone." The long waiting over, the weaver has finished the final garment, her shroud. "Her foot has grown still/On the treadle of doom."

Bow Down in Jericho, published in 1950, also includes ballads. This time the subjects are biblical: songs of Elijah drawn from II Kings 2 and "Remembrance of Moab" from the story of Ahab in II Kings 3. Charming and poignant indeed are the three ballads that tell of the meeting and parting of the friends, David and Jonathan. There are larks at the meeting of the two, raucous crows at the sad parting when Jonathan's father, Saul, has become angered with David and has exiled the young shepherd from the house. Reece winds up this moving sequence with "The Remembrance of Jonathan," which reflects the line, "Jonathan hath yet a son," from II Samuel 9:3. After David has become King of Israel, he looks out at one "feasting at his board who...by the look that he had on, (reminds) the king of Jonathan."

With the recognition that soared following the publication of *The Ballad of the Bones,* Reece began to receive many invitations from around the state of Georgia to read from his works. After short trips to Atlanta to appear at Druid Hills Baptist Church and to Gainesville to visit Brenau College, on April 13, 1946, Reece traveled two hundred miles to Macon to be guest of honor at the annual breakfast of the Macon Writers' Club. It was the longest journey the twenty-eight-year-old had made in his life. Shortly after that, on April 30th, Reece first met his supporter, Jesse Stuart, in person at the Book Fair in Atlanta.

The young poet was flattered by the invitations that poured in, but he soon discovered that public appearances interfered with his novel-in-progress and kept him from getting his farm work done. He also began to suspect that many who came to readings were mainly just curious to see what a mountain man looked like. His head was not turned by the attention. To a woman in Atlanta who remarked that he must surely have been named for the English poets Lord Byron and George Herbert, he replied, "No, it was for a butcher and an insurance salesman."

City life held no appeal for him. A deep love for all things growing and an even deeper sense of responsibility for his family's welfare were elements in the make-up of Reece, the farmer. His education at Young Harris College had been cut short by the necessity for him to tend the farm during the illness of his parents. For the rest of his life, although he was away from Wolf Creek for brief periods, he continued to plant and reap crops of corn and potatoes as well as to write his poems and two novels when the day's work was done.

The pursuit of both farming and writing was a continuing problem that the farmer/poet faced. An article written by Reece for *The Atlanta Journal* states the situation pretty succinctly:

> Once while I was writing my first novel, I happened to remark to a
> correspondent that I had been plowing potatoes. She wrote that I

should concentrate on the book. 'Anybody can plow potatoes,' she said. 'Anybody can plow potatoes,' I wrote in return, 'but nobody is willing to plow mine but me.'

Reece inherited a love for land passed down through generations of mountain farmers who had tilled the valleys of Union County since before the Cherokees were driven out of Georgia in 1838. Rich soil in the lowlands beside Wolf Creek, the steep rise of Blood Mountain and its dark timbered slopes, these were the source of the poet's identity. When he was teaching in California he wrote: "This is not my climate really. I think I'll have to get back on the ground, North Georgia and vicinity, before I can do much on the novel." And in a 1952 letter to Elliott Graham at E.P. Dutton, he described the struggles of his dual roles: "I still work the farm on Wolf Creek, and I often find myself over-extended and feeling very much akin to the insect known to all children as a 'grandaddy' who must have trouble figuring out which way he is going since his legs point in all directions at once." Both pursuits, he said, "make too many demands on your energy and time." There were times, both before and after the diagnosis of tuberculosis, when he had strength for neither.

Whatever the struggle in the poet's mind concerning his two vocations, the richness of the poetic metaphor is gleaned from the involvement of his five senses with the land of his home area. In late 1945, he sent a poem to *The Progressive Farmer* which sums up the farmer in the poet:

IF GOD SHOULD NEED ME

If God should need me, He knows
    where to look.
I'll be in the field with the mountains
    tall behind me,
Plowing the rows that dip their feet
    in the brook;
From May to July that is where He'll
    find me.
And after that, who better than God
    should know
How rank the numberless weeds and
    elderberries
Grow on the creek banks for my blade
    to mow –
He'll find me down by the water that
    loiters and hurries.
September dawns I'll be in the fields
    again,

Stripping the corn blades from the
    stalks that rustle
In every little wind. The sowing of
    grain
And the cribbing of corn will make me
    hurry and hustle
Throughout November. Should God
    seek me then
And come to my house He might find
    me within.

Reece as man and writer was caught up in the mystery of life and the slow turning of seasons. The metaphor, image, or analogy of fully half of his poems, especially the lyrics, came from his observations of the hills and valleys of his homeland. Whether he is writing of love or hatred, joy or despair, he tells it in the brown rabbit hiding in the hedge near his cornfield, the wren and the mouse he saw in a house "abandoned by men." He is obsessed with the wind that blows down the sides of Blood Mountain, its "rough palm" remembered by the "meadows" of his mind. He speaks of the mower stunned by the "rainbow" created by early dew shining on his scythe and of evening's peace likened to a dove flying forth from the dovecote in the yard. His living eyes ponder corn "ripe in husky shields" in a dead man's fields, and night pressing so hard it must bring the mountain down.

He writes a sonnet bright with "amber corns" and yellow pumpkins near "corn as gold as any minted pelf." In another, the housewife counts a rosary of the fruits and vegetables which she has stored against the days when "northers whistle and the drifts pile high." To these and all things of the earth he speaks in the harmony of the turning seasons. In an essay entitled "By Many a Way," he writes: "Summer is the high point of the poetry seasons. Autumn is an elegy. Winter is epic and cold. In winter the spirit drinks water from a wooden bowl. In summer there is wine."

It is interesting to speculate that the poet and the farmer understood that the word "verse" originated in the turning of the furrows of a field. Thus the poet and the farmer must be in many ways inextricable, the one the nurturer of the other. As Reece plows the curving rows of the fields by Wolf Creek, he is listening to the sky above, the rocks beneath his feet, and he pledges his words to this kingdom which has no voice but his:

THE SPEECHLESS KINGDOM

Unto a speechless kingdom I
Have pledged my tongue, I have given my word
To make the centuries-silent sky
As vocal as a bird.

The stone that aeons-long was held
As mute through me has cried aloud
Against its being bound, has spelled
Its boredom to a crowd.

Of trees that leaned down low to hear
One with complaint so like their own
– I being to the trees an ear
And tongue to the mute stone.

And I being pledged to fashion speech
For all the speechless joy to find
The wonderful words that each to each
They utter in my mind.

The months following the publication of *Ballad of the Bones* (in 1946) were busy
ones. Reece was working some eighteen hours a day on the farm, writing more
poems, polishing the novel which would be called *Better a Dinner of Herbs,* and
answering letters from friends and well-wishers. Both his father and his mother
were increasingly weakened by the tuberculosis that plagued them and though
there was literary recognition, little cash flowed into the family coffers. At the
end of the summer of 1947, Reece became ill too, describing himself in a letter to
his friend Mildred Greear, wife of Philip, as being on "the verge of cracking up."

THREE "A Solitary Thing"

DESPITE THE HARDNESS of his life at this time, he was working pretty steadily on the novel during 1948 and 1949 as well as making a few trips into the literary world. At the invitation of Dr.William Tate, dean of students at the University of Georgia, he spent a brief period there. Away from home and illness, he read poems and spoke to classes of students.

The year 1950 saw the publication of the novel *Better a Dinner of Herbs*, as well as a second volume of poetry, *Bow Down in Jericho*. The reviews came in, as well as a feature article in *Newsweek*, and he began to hope that he might make enough money to afford his family a better living. The novel was well received in his home state, but reviews in New York and other cities ranged from "enthusiasm to confusion to disapproval." *The Saturday Review of Literature* praised Reece's "simplicity, honesty, and… almost Biblical reliance on the repeated image," balancing emotion with "desperate intent." The result, says the review, is "powerful and often beautiful." Reece, however, was not pleased; the review was too brief to satisfy him.

Returning home from a book promotion tour in Atlanta, exhausted and ill with influenza, he struggled with writing a second novel. The weather was bad and nothing much else could be done. "I am always torn between two loyalties, one to go on making bread on the farm and the other to get out of my system those things I want to comment on through writing," he wrote to Pratt Dickson, his California correspondent. "If I could earn a living through writing what I want to write, I'd be as happy as any mortal can expect to be. It is possible that I may be able to do that one time, but not yet."

In the poem, "I Go by Ways of Rust and Flame" (*Ballad of the Bones*), the poet describes not only the lonely life experienced by the dedicated writer, but the particular personality of this man as well. He calls himself "a solitary thing" and states that he will "walk alone as all men must." As Byron Reece was both drawn toward and frustrated by his love for the native hearth and soil, so it was with relationships with people. These feelings are evidenced both in his poetry and in the wide correspondence which he carried on during the years with such people as E.V. Griffith, Pratt Dickson, Marel Brown, and William Tate. In an undated letter to Dickson he wrote of the many people he could have loved if "I had had the time and the means and hadn't been too concerned with my own ego to do so."

Life was a lonesome road for Reece, and reading the four collections of poems, one encounters the lonely voice again and again. "Mankin's Song" (*A Song of Joy*) expresses the paradoxical "miserable and merry" quality of a life where "tears have all rippled into laughter... laughter has taggled into tears." "From the Road" asks the question: "What do you see as you travel the lonesome road?" and answers, "Little enough;/Familiar bird in the bush, familiar toad/As brown as snuff." Even these small things may only be held for a brief while before they, too, must be surrendered, "not with tears, with a smile." These smallest creatures, a mouse and a wren, fail to notice or care that a habitation of man has been abandoned in "Feathers and Fur" (*Bow Down in Jericho*). One speaker lives "On the Precipice" (*Bow Down in Jericho*), looking into the empty pit, but another finds some comfort in the thought that the fodder stack,"symbol of that season's yield" will be viewed "By Other Eyes" (*Bow Down in Jericho*) when the poet has been at rest a hundred years. In the much-quoted epigraph which Reece wrote for *Bow Down in Jericho*, he asks that his stories and rhymes should "engage some friendly tongue" when he is "past the reach of song."

That he, who was never married, understood the nature of romantic love between the sexes is reflected in poems such as "My True Love" (*The Season of Flesh*) which darkens the theme of the old folk song, "Black, Black is the Color of My True-Love's Hair." After the first and second stanzas of the poem praise the hair, lips and throat of the beloved, in the third stanza the relationship takes on a threatening tone as the beloved's fingers are "fiercer than brands/ And total a ten of terror." In the next four lines an allusion to Christ adds a destructive note. "My love for my True-Love is darker than death," says the final stanza. It goes on to speak of tasting the "Wine from my True-Love's lips" and the "Bread... my True-Love's body," but ends: "And the vinegar waits at my fingertips,/And the Cross stands hewn and ready." It would seem from these final images that the lover threatens to crucify the beloved, much as the jealous or vengeful lover threatens the life of the beloved in "Lest the Lonesome Bird" and other ballads.

In "The End of Love" (*The Season of Flesh*), the poet sees that "the least of love is error," and "the most of love is terror." But, having "ended a long love," he involves nature in the healing process by calling on the mourning dove to change his sad tune and the streams to dance and sing again. Nature, then, holds more lasting comfort than the ambiguities of human love.

"Song" (*A Song of Joy*) expresses the deep need for a lover to "tryst with me in shadow/When the wind blows over/The asters in the meadow", and, in a poem sent to Ralph McGill in 1954 and later published in *The New Orleans Poetry Journal*, "The Tree, the Bird, and the Leaf," a cry from the very heart envisions a nature that never withers, never ceases to sing. The final stanza is wistful:

> There is a dew on the leaf of the green tree
> Where the bird is thralled in song:
> In the shadow of the branches

It is morning all day long.
And morning should be forever
And the night should never fall
If my Love loved me as I love
If my Love loved me at all.

Love in the ballads reflects the traditional "domestic" tragedy themes so familiar to the reader of the Child Collection of English and Scottish ballads. "The Ballad of the Rider," praised by Jesse Stuart in his introduction to *Ballad of the Bones*, tells the story of Helmer, who, having lost his love, fares forth, knife in hand, to insure that if he may not have her "warmth by night" and "her bright look by day", then no other man may. The lyrical way in which the thwarted lover describes his lady to those who may have seen her on the way gradually builds up an incomparable portrait of one much beloved and lost. The ballad ends as the lover learns of the death of his lady. His knife finds home in his own breast as he fares forth again to seek her in the world "beyond."

Reece considers homosexual love in his poems about the Old Testament story of David and Jonathan. In a letter to Pratt Dickson, he states that his approach to this love, "not a strange thing in Canaan in those days, but frowned on in Israel," has been derived from his reading of the Old Testament books of Samuel, Judges, and Kings, as well as scholarly books. He comments on the beauty one scholar finds in the relationship and concludes: "Very well, then. But their relationship was Freudian all the same, a homosexual attachment, which is a different matter from saying their relationship was that of perverts, since the former phrase indicated only the direction of the id." Whatever the truth about David and Jonathan, Reece has written singing words in his ballads about these ancient friends.

Another kind of relationship with people is most clearly outlined in both poems and correspondence as the poet struggles with his ambivalent feelings toward teaching and students. As neither farming nor writing contributed much toward financial security, necessity often forced him into teaching. He did not feel "cut our for a teacher" and begrudged the time away from his writing. On the other hand, he wrote from California in 1957, "I miss my students." In the poem "In the Corridor" (*The Season of the Flesh*), he pictures a student turning at the door to look back at the professor who has just closed "the ponderous book on Herrick's song,/Caught still in the youthful music, caught in the spell/Of its sound on a youthful tongue."

The large collection of his teaching notes in the University of Georgia collection testifies to the many hours Reece spent in preparing his lectures. Those who found him somber and taciturn most of the time did not know the man whose face so lightened when he discussed the lyrics of William Shakespeare, Vachel Lindsay, or Edward Arlington Robinson.

This was a lonely man but perhaps that loneliness was the price he was willing to pay. In an article for *The Atlanta Journal Magazine* he spelled out the contracts that governed the days of his life:

> We all have to participate in some form of marriage in this life, and mine has been to farming and writing. The marriage contract is to love, honor and cherish through sickness and health. If a confession of bigamy is implicit in my figure of speech, I can only admit it, but like the poet Cynara I have been faithful to each in my fashion. I have dropped work on a story to do spring plowing when the hero was on the point of giving the villain his come-uppance. I have made the land wait for its harvest until I finished a book.

Reece and his father.
Date unknown.

FOUR "*A Singer of Rich and Lasting Songs*"

THE NEED FOR MONEY CONTINUED. The previous year had not been good for farming, and the illness of both parents continued. The old home was in sad condition, and Reece was building a new house nearby. With this financial situation in mind, in 1950 he accepted an invitation to teach during the summer term at the University of California in Los Angeles. He accepted with some misgivings, since all the experience he had of teaching was the short stint in the rural schools of Union County. Although he would have preferred to travel by bus and see the country, he flew to Los Angeles, knowing how tiring a bus trip would be. He did not tell his mother, who feared flying, that he had flown, not then, not ever.

He arrived in Los Angeles on June 19th. He taught a course in the short story and one on "Verse Writing" in the mornings; his afternoons were free for other pursuits. Whatever else may be said of the California experience, it is certain that he was not comfortable in the halls of academe. There, as when he was reading or lecturing to the public, he felt that he was on display as that oddity – the mountain man who writes. After his return to Choestoe, he wrote to E.V. Griffith about the "intellectuals who scorn anything simply stated and who have no belief in anything to pull themselves together." A few weeks later he wrote:

> Universities are such disappointing places because one demands that they fulfill his ideals for the university and they do not...I know that the measure of failure in such institutions is often the measure of the smallness of the men in them. Too, steeped as Americans are in the tradition of Success which means money and position and power, the universities just can't help treating the arts as a sort of step-child from which nothing much is expected.

To add to his distress, it was soon evident that his salary of $1120.40 would barely cover his travel and living expenses. Near the end of the summer, he was offered a fellowship by the Huntington Hartford Foundation for a three-month retreat at Pacific Palisades to finish a second novel (then entitled *Tents Toward Sodom*). He was tempted, but as the Foundation only paid living expenses, he asked for a postponement until his financial commitments at home were in better shape.

The best event of that summer was the release of *Bow Down in Jericho* in mid-July, followed by his public lecture on July 25 before a large audience at the university. The reviews of this second volume of poetry were generally good; one critic called Reece one of the important younger writers in America. *The Atlanta Constitution* columnist Harold Martin praised the biblical ballads, saying that they "sing like the call of rams' horns blowing from ancient battlements of the Holy Land." According to his biographer, Reece was considered for the Pulitzer prize in poetry. The records of the Pulitzer committee do not show that the book was nominated; it is possible that it did not make it through the screening process.

At the end of a very busy summer with little time for rest, in August Reece left Los Angeles to drive to Oklahoma City with an acquaintance, Roy Penny. He met with several literary groups there and gave a poetry reading. Then he returned home. This was the longest time that he would ever be absent from the familiar hills of Choestoe. In the previously mentioned letter to E.V. Griffith he wrote of the joys of being home, "The world here is so astonishingly beautiful one can hardly bear to look at it."

Bow Down in Jericho was doing well, and he went to Atlanta for an interview on WSB-Radio in December. Harold Martin saw him standing on the corner waiting for a bus, "tall, thin, bony, gaunt and lean…his bare head shaggy, his big hands burned by the sun and roughened by work in the field." He marveled that "at night in the little house where he lives with his father and mother, he writes some of the most beautiful lyric poetry…being written today."

Despite this and other fine reviews of *Jericho*, monetary success still eluded him. In a letter to E.V. Griffith he daydreamed about buying a new radio and record changer. "Then I'll buy all of the Beethoven I can afford, some Mozart, Schubert, and Bach." These were the favorites which the poet would mention any time the subject of music came into conversation or correspondence.

Recognition continued during 1950. In June he was given the highest awards for both poetry and fiction by the Georgia Writers Association. The Literary Achievement Award citation for poetry read in part: "…we wish to acknowledge the work of a writer of brilliant dimensions, a young singer of rich and lasting songs whose pen is making a profound impression on the world of provocative and long remembered literature."

In spite of much acclaim in literary circles and from critics across the country, book sales continued to be disappointing. By 1951, the critical illness of his father made the burden of all the farm work fall upon the son. Reece had made little progress on the second novel and found it necessary to ask for an extended deadline from E.P. Dutton. He applied for a Guggenheim fellowship, although his feeling that this was some form of charity was a real problem for the proud and independent mountain man. In the meantime, honors flowed in. At the

Georgia Press Institute meeting in Athens he read "The Weaver," which would be included in the next volume of poetry, A *Song of Joy*, published in 1952. In April he received a Guggenheim fellowship with its award of three thousand dollars. It could not have come at a better time.

It is poignant to consider that with the heavy problems weighing down the young poet he could state in the title poem:

> Saying, how better
>   Could I employ
> The tittle of my time
>   Than in searching for joy?

The poet is, indeed, searching for joy, and on that search he encounters priest, sage, those who suffer, and other travelers whose constant companion is Death. The pain of the poet's struggle with life is nowhere more apparent than in this third volume of his poems.

Again the reviews were generally good. In the *Los Angeles Times*, a reviewer identified as "P.T.S." observed, "This reader likes a poet that compels him to dance; that inspires him to chant aloud; a poet that charms him to the marrow of his bones. And that is why he commends, with more than the ordinary assurance and gusto, the poems of Byron Herbert Reece."

Not all reviewers praised him. George Scarborough felt the poet's preoccupation with death was excessive. Sara Henderson Hay in *The Saturday Review* accused him of being too derivative, mentioning such poets as Davies, Millay, Frost, and Blake. This review evoked angry letters from the poet both to the publisher and to the magazine. He wrote to *The Saturday Review*:

> Until I read Sara Henderson Hay's review of my recent book…I was totally unaware of my apparently stupendous powers of mimicry. I would submit, if I were not too angry to do so, that to be able to imitate every name poet since the middle of the 17th century is to exhibit no mean gift…her charges…are so unfounded they are, if not actually so, perilously close to malicious…The effect of Miss Hay's review is to mutilate my integrity as a writer.

To add insult to injury, he adds, the editors of the magazine have "abetted" in the insult by captioning his photograph, "Byron H. Reece – candidly derivative."

At the end of a summer of hard farm work, illness, and little progress on the second novel, Reece agreed to teach at his alma mater, Young Harris College, for the fall quarter. He was "broke as a hant" and must commute daily to tend his ill parents. It was not a happy situation in many ways. In October he wrote to E.V. Griffith about the time-consuming task of grading papers and rereading

text materials he had not encountered for fifteen years. His publisher was anx-
ious to have the completed manuscript and "besides, when I get thirty or forty
papers to read and grade answers to questions nobody has any business being
asked anyway, I think: My God, what am I doing here? Of course the answer is
I'm doing it for money which is not a very good reason for teaching." In the
press of academic work he was cheered in October by a fourth award from the
Georgia Writers Association, and on December 1, the poet/teacher presented
his award plaque for A Song of Joy to the college.

FIVE "A Chronicle in Hell"

BY THE END OF THE SCHOOL QUARTER, Reece was feeling so dizzy and weak that he went to see his doctor, already guessing that the verdict would be the same tuberculosis that had attacked both his parents. He wrote later to William Tate: "I was awfully sensitive about it at first, but I've come to realize a spade by any other name is still a spade." He entered the state hospital for the tubercular on February 8, 1954, for a stay of three months, later described in "A Chronicle in Hell." In "Underground" which is included in the final book of poetry, *The Season of Flesh*, he recalls Battey State Hospital:

> In that subterranean city
> To which I came at last
> A ghost walked, and was pity,
> And the ghost walked past and past,
> At the middle bells, at midnight,
> Help! cried a bundle of bones.

Bones, indeed, for when he walked out of the hospital early in May, more gaunt than ever, he weighed only one hundred twenty-five pounds.

The problems had been many. Although the state institution was free, the expenses at home continued. He lost an opportunity to spend time at Emory University as poet-in-residence. Added to all that, the novel remained unfinished. These worries combined to make his stay in the hospital an uneasy one. "Things have been getting beyond me for a long while," he confided in a letter to his friends the Greears, "I ran out of energy and then ran on for a year or so… This place is difficult to take. I am about as unhappy here as I have ever been in my life."

Concerned about the situation at home and about his writing, Reece left the hospital in May, saying that he would rather die than return. He did promise his doctors that he would take the prescribed medicine and rest at home. In June, X-rays showed that the spots on his lungs were beginning to heal and he began to feel somewhat less depressed. By July, he had finished the manuscript of *The Season of Flesh* and dedicated the volume of poems to a former student, Barry Williams. The dedicatory poem seems to contradict some of his complaints about teaching. Here both subject and student appear in a much softer light:

IN THE CORRIDOR

Clouds I remember, a day all dull and dun;
The sun may have shone at the first for a little space,
I do not remember. Clouds I remember, and one

Figure departing, one grave unsmiling face.

The voice reading ceased at the sound of the bell
And I closed the ponderous book on Herrick's song,
Caught still in the youthful music, caught in the spell
Of its sound on a youthful tongue.

The door of that classroom fronts on an open hall
And one may go by the way he came, or not;
But this was the eve of holiday for all
And from my desk I followed the laughing lot.

Just where the hallway opens upon the street
One looked back for a moment, as if to find
Whether my gaze sought his, and, should they meet,
Whether my mind

Was still for the ageless music of Herrick, or
For the aging day, or the book,
Or for the face at the end of the corridor
And its fleeting backward look.

The Season of Flesh was published in 1955. In the same year the finally-finished novel, which told the grim story of the lynching of Dandelion, a black man wrongly accused of violating a white woman, appeared with the title *The Hawk and the Sun*.

Reece's mother had died on August 30, 1954. Since she had been the one who had most encouraged his writing career, it was a more-than-usual season of grief for the poet. It was, then, in the midst of illness, grief, and depression that he finished his last two books.

The Hawk and the Sun received a mixed bag of responses, as Reece had known it would. One critic called it the "ugliest [most] perverted blend of human degradation." On the other hand, the *Los Angeles Times* review by Paul Jordan-Smith found the novel was "clothed in beauty and moves with grace, so that the ugly and the cruel are seen clearly for precisely what they are." Of the forty reviews which Reece had seen by mid-October, most were favorable.

The Season of Flesh, on the other hand, received more praise than the three earlier volumes of poetry. One reviewer called Reece "one of the greatest U.S. poets." "I know of no living poet writing in the English language, or pretending to, who has written lyrics equal to the best poems in *The Season of Flesh* by Byron Herbert Reece," wrote Edward M. Case, a syndicated critic. "It seems to me that with the exception of Robert Frost, Reece is our greatest living poet, and even Frost is not so pure a lyricist, nor as strong and lonely as voice."

Such high praise, however, seemed to make little difference to Reece. Even though his lung appeared to be healing, he did not feel well. Health and money worries, depression and grief were aggravated by the mixed reaction to *The Hawk and the Sun*. The fact that so many found the book offensive added to the already heavy burden that he carried in the fall of 1955. "I have written nothing since the last day of 1954, when I completed the manuscript of *The Hawk and the Sun*," he wrote to Pratt Dickson in May, 1957. "I doubt if I ever write much more poetry. I don't feel it anymore."

By the fall of 1956, his doctors cautiously agreed that Reece might accept an invitation to spend the winter quarter at Emory University. He hoped that the job would not be too taxing, writing to Pratt Dickson: "I'll have the title of Poet in Residence, and so be relieved of the pretensions toward scholarship a professor must have. I have a distinct distaste for all classroom work, but I guess I can manage for a quarter at the salary they offer."

The course proved to be so popular that registration had to be closed long before all the students who wanted to take it had been admitted. Notebooks of lecture notes for the class (now in the University of Georgia collection) indicate a rich experience. "You might expect this poet to be a taciturn farmer," commented Celestine Sibley in *The Atlanta Constitution*, but "you should hear him talk." Remembering Reece as teacher, many former students would contrast the melancholy man who walked the campus paths and the teacher who "lit up" when he spoke on his favorite subject.

The course at Emory and the demands of people who may not have known how fragile his health was took their toll. By the end of the quarter, he had lost weight, was spitting blood, and altogether was too ill to consider returning in the spring quarter.

Back home, he tried to rest and regain some of the lost ground. He had signed a contract for the first novel of a trilogy which would be based on the history of the Georgia-North Carolina mountain area. Again in financial need, he put back his pride and applied for a second Guggenheim to fund his research. He was trying to push his weakness back into creativity, but in June of 1956, he wrote in deep discouragement to Elliot Graham:

> There was a pretty good book...called *The Folded Leaf*.... Anyway the boy who cut his throat discovered that each man has his limit. Beyond this wall I may not go, each man says to himself somewhere along the line. Well, I've just reached my wall. I've reached the absolute limit of my energy. I couldn't do more than I'm doing if my life depended on it. That's all there is to it. I think perhaps you might be right in thinking things would work out in time. But wait-

ing it out is a luxury that I can't afford anymore. Success and I just missed connections somewhere along the line. Well, to hell with it. I've got to eat. I don't like to be hungry. So I'll meet my English classes as long as I can.

He taught that summer at Young Harris College, and continued there throughout the 1956-57 school year. As he no longer had the strength to raise crops on the farm, teaching seemed the only answer to the financial problems that continued to plague him.

In November of 1956, Reece received yet another Literary Achievement Award from the Georgia Writers Association for *The Season of Flesh*, and in May of the following year he received a Guggenheim fellowship to work on the projected trilogy of mountain novels. This enabled him to spend the summer months at the Huntington Hartford Foundation in California, taking up the resident fellowship which he had deferred several years before. In September, he returned to Choestoe and began a part-time teaching appointment at Young Harris.

Friends and colleagues at the college remember that he was "more withdrawn and nervous...had developed a tremor...and showed a sense of panic at the thought of meeting strangers." A colleague in the English department told of watching him, trying to keep him from being too much alone. Speaking of his suicide, she said: "It was not so much a question of if, only of when." Even so, he excelled as a teacher. A student who was in his class that year told Raymond Cook, "He was a professor who had a way of appealing to the creative ability of the student, and he drew out of the student his hidden potential which someone else may not have been able to do."

Reece managed to live out the school year, but in the spring of 1958, just at graduation time, he put a bullet through his diseased lungs in the same campus apartment where his beloved mentor, Dr. Lufkin Dance, had killed himself in 1946. When concerned colleagues and students found him, Mozart's *Piano Sonata in D* was still playing on his phonograph. In his desk drawer, his last student papers, all graded, had been left in a neat stack.

Conclusion

THE POET IS BURIED near his mother's grave in Old Union Cemetery at the edge of the small town of Young Harris. Tributes poured in from those who had known the man, his work, or both. In an editorial in *The Atlanta Constitution*, Reece's long-time friend Ralph McGill expressed his sense of loss and quoted from a poem which the poet had written many years earlier:

> I give my love to earth, where I
> A longer, deeper sleep will take
> Than when woken from when the night is by,
> As I lie down to wake.
>
> To earth I give my love, my love;
> I give my love to earth to keep
> Against the time, with earth above
> When I lie down to sleep.

Truly here was a sensitive poet, an inspiring teacher. In his ballads and lyrics praising the warm soil of his native Choestoe, he left a legacy of thoughtful lines natural to one who had spent his life in the closest communion with the oak tree and wild ginger, squirrels and the shy deer that roam the slopes of Blood Mountain. To those who had known him, friend and student alike, he left memories of lectures, letters, and conversations rich with the thoughts of the great writers of the past. And Reece left, for later readers, six books which continue to be read and studied, for the rich cadences revealing his love for the King James Bible, for his ceaseless probing into the nature of the human condition, and for the homely images and metaphors that move both heart and mind. No finer tribute exists than that with which Dr. Raymond Cook closes his fine biography, *The Mountain Singer: The Life of Byron Herbert Reece*:

> ...whenever men retreat to quiet vales of the mind to seek a lifting
> of the heart in friendship, a warm joy in simple things, and a catch-
> ing of the breath at supernal beauty, there the lonely, questing spirit
> of Byron Herbert Reece will have found a haven, and his haunting
> flute-like music will be heard.

Reece presents his
fourth Georgia Writers
Association award to
Young Harris College
president Charles Clegg
and head librarian
Florence Tolar.

Discussion Questions

1. Reece is described by his principal and English teacher to be a shy individual. Is this characteristic reflected in his poetry, in your opinion? Explain.

2. Do you think there is any contradiction in the statement that he didn't care if people recognized his poetry and the evidence that he made considerable efforts (often successful) to be published?

3. Sellers remarks that Ralph McGill saw a physical resemblance between Reece and Abraham Lincoln. Beyond this physical resemblance, do you see other similarities in the words and writings of these men? Explain.

4. If you learned that there was to be a reading of Reece's poetry in your community, would you try to attend?

5. Malcolm Sumner, Regent's Professor and agronomist at the University of Georgia, has defined soil to be "where life meets death in an exchange of energy." How do you think Reece would respond to this definition?

6. Do you think Reece's vacillating feelings about teaching are typical of most people who teach young adults? Explain.

7. Sellers' story of Reece's life describes many forms of hardship – ailing parents, farm work, little money, not enough time. Do you think these hardships positively or negatively influenced his writings? Explain.

8. The videotape presents several traditional poetic themes, for example, love, death, immortality, friendship, isolation, loneliness, nature, time, life seasons, beauty. Which of these themes, or others, held the most meaning for you as you watched the video?

9. Is this poet someone you would have wanted to know personally? Why or why not?

10. Do you think the poetry would be attended by young adults today as they are portrayed listening to Reece on the video?

11. How would you describe Reece's view of religion? Do you think this is a common view of persons who live in relatively isolated agrarian communities?

12. Reece mentions that he came "close to death" three times during his lifetime. Do you think these "near death" experiences influenced the ideas and emotions he presented in his poetry? Explain.

13. Reece said that people who cannot appreciate poetry miss part of their heritage. Would you concur? If so, can you think of poems that are particularly meaningful in this way?

14. The poet seems secure in his opinion that a writer, rural or urban, must isolate himself or herself in order to write. Based upon your knowledge of writers, do you agree?

15. Did the cinematography and acting in the video contribute to your appreciation of the poetry, or did you find it distracting? Explain.

16. How did you react to his critique of modern poetry, especially his comments that he did not appreciate poets who would make an effort to be deliberately obscure?

17. Reece appears to have had some strong views on most ideas he addresses in his poetry. For example, he mentions "no hope in heaven, logically or theologically," and he tells us that he does not believe in just the possibility of one love, but of many loves. Of all the issues introduced in this video, which would you want to discuss in more depth?

Poems for Discussion

"Mother lay the fire again
And put the kettle on the stove;
The hills are curtained by the rain,
And I have lost my love."

"Son, the fire leaps in the grate,
The kettle whistles through its spout,
And supper on the board will wait
Until your story's out."

"Well, Mother, yesterday I saw
My loved one walking the hills,
Twining roses in her hair
And picking daffodils."

"And there was nothing strange in that.
Had she no word to say to you
That you go like an angry cat
The whole day through?"

"No, Mother, ere the hills became
Green with the young leaf I was lost
By looking on a colder flame
Than burns at the heart of frost.

"And yesterday I saw my love
With another lover in the wood,
And who but I should walk with her
In the green solitude?

"I could not bear to see her bend
Her lips to another's wooing,
And it was never friend and friend
That kissed as they were doing."

"Stranger things were done, my son;
Nothing may come of it at last;
So let your head see what is done;
The heart runs too fast."

"The heart too fast and the feet too fast
And the hands too fast to slaughter-
Someone seeks in the woods so vast
Tonight, for a lost daughter.

"And, Mother, lest the lonesome bird
Haunt me from the willow,
I made her a prayer that no one heard
And gave her a stone for a pillow.

"Mother, listen to the rain
That slashes ever harder-
Her handsome lover have I slain
And left him there to guard her.

"Mother, listen to the night
That howls about the eaves-
I hid them well and out of sight
With many little leaves.

"Mother, hush and tend the fire
And lay the bed with a clean cover
I sleep tonight with a new desire,
With a dread and faithful lover."

Of the more than thirty ballads included in the four volumes of Reece's poems, about half are based on biblical themes. The others follow closely the patterns and themes common to the ballads brought to this country from various parts of the British Isles. Reece was well versed in the ballad stanza, a form having roughly six or eight beats to the short line and rhyming first line with third, second line with fourth. Each ballad, whether traditional or biblical, will tell a story of sorts.

"Lest the Lonesome Bird" follows the traditional theme of broken love and tragedy with the ending implying either an early death for the murdering lover or, at the very least, a strong sense of damnation for his deed.

A point to consider in this ballad is the nature of "the lonesome bird." What are the possibilities of identification for this symbol?

Examine the poem for details that seem natural to Reece's hill country.

WHOSE EYE IS ON THE SPARROW

I saw a fallen sparrow
Dead upon the grass
And mused to see how narrow
The wing that bore it was.
By what unlucky chance
The bird had come to settle
Lopsided near the fence
In sword grass and nettle

I had no means to know;
But this I minded well:
Whose eye was on the sparrow
Shifted, and it fell.

This poem, assuming some knowledge of the passage in Matthew 10:29-31, was first published in *The Enotah Echoes*, the campus newspaper at Young Harris College. Here the young poet hints at his concept of religious faith with an approach that he would follow throughout his life and writing career.

How do you see Reece's concept of divine providence? Is his idea of divine providence the traditional one?

Has the poet used the sparrow, common in North Georgia, because of the biblical reference?

How does this poem reflect on Reece's familiarity with the Bible?

O ELEMENTS

I who must bear the ceaseless rage
Of constant war with time, engage
Always the foe, therefore to see
The sun at morn is victory.

Seeking alliances, I plead
With all things succoring my need,
And count it nothing less than right
The elements by my side should fight.

O Sun, when time has conquered me
Diminished shall your rising be,
Or if my death by day be met
Direly depleted shall you set.

Consider, Air, when I shall keep
A silence death-ordained and deep,
By so much less shall be your note
As shakes the lyre-box of my throat.

O wayward Water, running down
With vocal flow by field and town,
Remember, when with death I go
Lessened shall all your currents flow.

Now, therefore, be for armament
And moat repelling death's advent
O Air and Water. Be, O Sun,
The signal yet of victory won.

What elements of the universe does the speaker in the poem address?

Does this remind you of the ancient invocations of earth, air, fire, and water – the basic elements that represent the totality of life?

Does the speaker plead for life or death – and what effect does he expect if he should die?

Think of English poet John Donne's "Meditation": "Each man's death diminishes me...ask not then for whom the bell tolls, it tolls for thee."

THE SPEECHLESS KINGDOM

Unto a speechless kingdom I
Have pledged my tongue. I have given my word
To make the centuries-silent sky
As vocal as a bird.

The stone that aeons-long was held
As mute through me has cried aloud
Against its being bound, has spelled
Its boredom to a crowd

Of trees that leaned down low to hear
One with complaint so like their own
– I being to the trees an ear
And tongue to the mute stone.

And I being pledged to fashion speech
For all the speechless joy to find
The wonderful words that each to each
They utter in my mind.

In this poem, what role does the poet see for himself?

To what elements of nature does he owe this service?

In citing the sky, the stone, the trees, has the poet chosen well from the natural world around him?

Would you consider this role sufficient for the whole body of work of a poet?

What else might he also give voice to?

THREE TIMES ALREADY I HAVE OUTWITTED DEATH

Three times already I have outwitted death;
He came to me first when I was a tender age
But I tore his hand from my mouth to drink in breath;
And again when winter was whirling in windy rage
He touched my lips with fingers blue as an aster
But could not stop my breath from coming and going;
And again he followed me fast, but I ran faster,
Out of the sea before the tide's inflowing.

Again and again will death prove troublesome;
He in his proximate passing will pluck at me
And I evade his grasp. But the time will come
When he will creep upon me and I not see,
Then he will pluck my life, as a leaf from a tree
Between the wind's keen, cold forefinger and thumb.

In what way or ways does the poet describe Death? In lines 4-5? Later, in the final three lines of stanza one?

Does the final image of Death, in the last two lines of the poem, have some connection with the image in lines 4-5?

Does the connection that the poet makes with Death fit with your view of his close communion with the natural world that surrounds him in North Georgia?

Reece, in the film, comments: "Aster is the frost flower." How does this statement add meaning to line 5?

Additional Poems

BALLAD OF THE BONES
Ezekiel, 37: 1-10

I

As I sat a-drowse
At my very meek board,
Why, who should arouse
Me from my sleep but the Lord.

He entered my garret
As a wind from the north,
And in the spirit
Carried me forth

Over town and town
Of cobbles and stones,
And He sat me down
In a valley of bones.

The bones were as dry
As grass in a drought,
And He said: "Pass by
Them round about."

And I passed by
And the white bones lay
As brittle and dry
As shards of clay.

And I passed by
And the bones were strewed
Brittle and dry,
And a multitude.

Shin bones here
And thigh bones there,
And arm bones, sere,
And skull bones, bare!

II

O I stood alone
At this very large grave
Where bone from his bone
Was fugitive
And the Lord: "Ezekiel,
Can these bones live?"

My mind's *ha, ha!*
Had a scornful ring,
But I clamped my jaw
On such a thing!

Shall a bone that has lain
Till the flesh is gone
Be quickened again
To a living bone?

Bones bent like an bow
And fugitive?
I thought, *no, no*
They cannot live!

But I bowed my head
And my thoughts in accord,
And trembled and said:
"Thou knowest, Lord!"

III

I shook, as the wind
Of the Lord went blowing,
As boneless and blind
As water flowing;

But His voice said
When the blow was by:
"Lift up thy head
And prophesy.

"Thou raiser of stones
To the power of death,
Say unto these bones,
'Ye shall draw your breath!'"
I said to the bones:
"Ye shall draw your breath!"

"Thou shaker of thrones
By the power I give,
Speak unto these bones
That they may live!"
I said to the bones:
"Thy God says, live!"

"Soothsayer of men,
Say on, say on,
Call flesh and skin
To cover the bone!"
I said: "Flesh, skin,
Come, cover the bone!"

"Ezekiel,
My Truth, My Rod,
These bones shall live
To call me God!"

IV

Something stirred
And I lost my voice;
I heard, I heard
A little noise!

I heard small moans
As the wind would make,
And I looked-and the bones
Began to shake!

As dry as faggots
And dull and dun,
And thick as maggots
In carrion,

With the sound of wind
In icy weather
The bones came rattling
All together!

From among the stones
As dark as soot,
The little bones
To make a foot,

With nought to teach
Them to their place,
Came each to each
In an empty space!

And from the stones,
As clean as a peg,
The larger bones
To make a leg!

The strangest sight
Since the world began,
The bones all right
To make a man!

V

When all the skeletons
Were done
The busy bones
Grew still again.

As a wood they were
When winter grieves
In the branches bare
Of the shape of leaves.

To give them strength
Then nerve and thew,
Length by length
And two by two,

With a snaky tread
And not a sound
Began to thread
Each bone around!
I hid my face,

I shut my eyes
For the little space
The heart beats thrice,

And then I looked
Again and saw
What is not brooked
By natural law:

Each skull a face,
And trunk and limb
Had the sweet grace
Of flesh on them!

   VI

But as I would praise
The miracle
A heavy haze
About me fell.

From the luminous mist
God's voice said:
"They with flesh are dressed,
But they are dead,

"And none can make
Them live but I;
Cease now to quake
And prophesy.

"To the four winds call,
Thou son of man,
That these slain may all
Draw breath again!"

I stood appalled
At His presence hid,
But I called, I called
As I was bid.

From hill and wood
Did the four winds meet,
And the slain all stood
Upon their feet;

An exceeding army,
They drew their breath
And stepped forth free
From the ranks of death!

   VII
Ezekiel,
Behold the blood
Of My sons that fall
In the world's dark wood!

Now prophesy
To the troubled host
Whose bones are dry,
Whose hope is lost;

In the battle's shock,
In the ways they grope,
I am their Rock,
I am their Hope!

Their blood I see,
I hear their groans,
Yea, and I am He
That raised the bones!

I: FOR BOW DOWN IN JERICHO

From chips and shards, in idle times,
I made these stories, shaped these
    rhymes;
May they engage some friendly tongue
When I am past the reach of song.

I GO BY WAYS OF RUST
AND FLAME

I GO by ways of rust and flame
Beneath the bent and lonely sky;
Behind me on the ways I came
I see the hedges lying bare,
But neither question nor reply.

A solitary thing am I
Upon the roads of rust and flame
That thin at sunset to the air.
I call upon no word nor name,
And neither question nor reply
But walk alone as all men must
Upon the roads of flame and rust.

INVOCATION

O SONG, hung as clear in the mind
As the tremor of beaten bells,
Come forth now, lovely and clear,
And undisturbed by the swells
Of the ocean of thought that beats
On the shores of a troubled year.
Let what the tongue repeats
Of evil and death be drowned
By a lovelier sound.

WE COULD WISH THEM
A LONGER STAY

Plum, peach, apple and pear
And the service tree on the hill
Unfold blossom and leaf.
From them comes scented air
As the brotherly petals spill.
Their tenure is bright and brief.

We could wish them a longer stay,
We could wish them a charmed bough
On a hill untouched by the flow
Of consuming time; but they

Are lovelier, dearer now
Because they are soon to go,
Plum, peach, apple and pear
And the service blooms whiter than
    snow.

THE SOUND OF RAIN

I said to myself beneath the roof
One rainy night while fast they fell
From clouds with many in store for
    proof:
What raindrops most resemble tell.
The answer that my fancy gave,
Since it could say the thing it chose:
I think the rain sounds like a wave
As sucking down the shore it goes.

The rain was always like the sea,
I told my fancy, try again.
And then my fancy said to me:
A lot of sticks are like the rain,
A lot of sticks cut from the brakes
Of cane that by the river crowd,
And set in rows like slender stakes
With top ends reaching to the cloud.

THE STAY-AT-HOME

The fields of Hughly held him,
The land where he was born.
With fence to mend and cows to tend
And care of wheat and corn
He had no lief to wander
Beyond his place of birth.
But often he would ponder
The luring lands of earth.

He loved the fields of Hughly
And every hill that stood
To bind him in with other men
Like him in bone and blood,
Who often thought of going
But had the will to stay
And turn them to their hoeing
When cocks crew up the day.

Yet, as the gypsy-hearted
Hearken when distance sings,
The sounds he most regarded
Were all of passing things:
Swift waters flowing,
Winds to westward blowing,
Footsteps outward going
And wild, wandering wings.

THERE NEVER WAS TIME

I wish, he said, the years would linger
And fly less fast to make me old;
My face is a mask that time's swift finger
Models, moulding wrinkle and fold
In sagging flesh youth fashioned true
To the ageless image, engraved on brass,
Of a young face Rome or Athens knew.
(There was time for youth to pass.)

Time had a long look when I was twenty;
Was there anything I had not done
And yet would do? Well, there was plenty
Of daylight left in the cycling sun.
The roughs of knowledge that wanted scaling
Loomed-there was time to be a sage;
Time and to spare to heal all ailing.
(And time enough for a man to age.)

But now the night that has no breaking
Shadows the sun gone down the west,
And my heart in its damaged cage is aching
After lost years, too brief at best.
I know a journey that yet wants going,
I know a song that is still to sing,
I know a fallow that waits the sowing-
(There never was time for everything.)

ELBOWS ON THE SKY

If a man might lean his elbows on the sky
As farmers lean their weight upon a wall
To look upon their ample fields that lie
Heavy with harvest in the yellow Fall,
Then he might dicker with close-fisted fate,
Himself decide what to reject or keep
Before he comes at length beyond the gate
Where he may choose not anything but sleep.

Yet if he leaned but once upon a star
And saw his earth, and himself fugitive,
As long as breath could keep life's door ajar
He would be happy but to breathe and live,
With little care for what he shall be when
Of death's gray waste he is a citizen.

IN ABSENCE

I call in the cold and silence, I speak your name
And hear no answer but echo, and ache with grief.
Find me in fire, for love, in the flickering flame
Fed by fagot and leaf.

Whenever the rose lifts resolute in spring
Find me, for love, in each unfolding petal;
In the greening leaf, in every living thing
Know me a little.

Breathe me, for love, in breathing the common air;
Of spirit or matter, of all things find me part.
Greet me in absence, for love, for I am there;
And in your heart

Keep me, O Love, as near as the constant flood
Washing its chambers. Wear me, for warmth, as close
In the channels of ivory mazing your leaping blood
As your warm blood flows.

BITTER BERRY

The voice of the water
Crying on a stone
Said to Helmer's daughter
Sitting alone:

"Death itself is mellow
When age has ripened one,
But death's a bitter berry
In the morning of the sun."

And so to Helmer's daughter,
The youngest one of all,
The green untimely berry
Was as bitter as gall.

NOW THAT SPRING IS HERE

Now that the year's advanced to spring
And leaves grow large and long
Forget each sorry and rueful thing
Hearing the wild bird's song.

The leaf will fall, the bird will fly
And winter close the year,
But O, put all such knowledge by
Now that spring is here!

45

BALLAD OF THE WEAVER

OLD Margot, the weaver,
Grows slow at the loom
As the thread flies over
The shuttle of doom.

Her fingers have guided
The pearly wool thread
That shroud has provided
The long-sleeping dead.

Her quick foot has treadled,
Her brown fingers styled
The warm cloth that swaddled
The new-crying child.

She has spun in the harness
Cloth, lovely and wide,
White gowning to bless
The first night of the bride.

And jeans she has woven,
For many a groom,
Whose thread is spun thin on
The shuttle of doom.

To curtain the vision
Of love, new and kind,
The cloth of derision
She wove in her mind.

And yet as she fingers
The bright, flowing thread
Her spinning thought lingers
With the lost or the dead,

With pains to discover
The rapture she knew
When night did not cover
One sleeper, but two.

Her cat hardly stirs
To be hearing again
The fall of her tears
Like a thin summer rain.

He knows from much telling
How when she was young
One came to her dwelling
With a smile and a song.

She loved him for graces
The traveler knows,
And for dust of far places
That clung to his clothes.

And all to discover
What many have known:
Whose lord is a rover
Her house keeps alone.

He rode from her humming
A tune full of tears;
And she waited his coming
And counted the years

That she had waited,
And he not come,
Till five had freighted
Each finger and thumb.

She speaks through the whirring
Of shuttle and thread,
And the cat, on hearing,
Has lifted his head:

"The thread is thinning;
My shroud is spun;
The weaving and spinning
Are over and done!"

The thread of her will
Has snapped in the loom;
Her foot has grown still
On the treadle of doom.

THE LARKS AT THE MEETING
OF DAVID AND JONATHAN

I

David the shepherd boy
From Bethlehem sped
To the host of Israel
With a few loaves of bread,

His harp at his shoulder,
Psalms in his throat,
And cheese from the milkings
Of an old she-goat.

He spoke with his brothers,
His song rang blithe,
And he took a stone and flung it
And killed Goliath!

As soon as he was come
From that fray with victory
King Saul said to Abner:
"Whose son is *he?*

"Go bid him forth."
And so David went
From his brothers to the king.
When he came to Saul's tent

Puffed as a toad
With what he had done,
His heart skipped a beat
When he looked on Jonathan.

O were I the brother
Of such an one, he said
And stared while his vision
Of the king and glory fled.

And a lark in a thicket
And a lark in a cloud
Sang both together
As those two bowed.

So the son of Jesse
And Jonathan
Found each other
In the morning of the sun.

Jonathan
Was the son of the King,
And David was a shepherd
With a harp and a sling,

But fair as a lily
And lithe was he,
And the color of roses
And ivory.

David was a harper
And his harping was fair
Till he looked on the king's son
Through a mist of cloudy hair.

His harp had then
A voice of its own
And what it played then
was *Jonathan.*

David was a psalmist
With a golden tongue,
But he looked on the king's son
And he forgot his song.
He looked on the king's son
And he forgot to sing,
Then his heart was strung
With a single throbbing string

And the tune of love
That string played on
Was *Jonathan, Jonathan*
Jonathan.

O, thought David
As he gazed his fill
When I watched the sheep
High on some lonely hill

Would that we together
Had woke and slept;
O that we together
The watch might have kept.

His hand on my shoulder
Perilous and kind,
And the little lambs playing
And baa-ing on the wind!

And the lark sang to David
From low in his mind,
And the lark sang to David
From a thicket twined.

II
David was a shepherd
Lithesome and tall
But Jonathan
Was the son of Saul.

A hero of battles,
The doughty Jonathan
Was the hope of the people
And king Saul's son.

Now what should the son
Of the king of Israel
Have in his heart
A shepherd lad to tell?

"As I would clothe me, even,
Against the rain and sun
Here is my robe, David,
For thee to put on.

("For surely I shall carry
Till my days are no more
The image of David
At my heart's still core.)

"As I would arm me, even,
To warrior for my Lord
Here is my blade, David,
Buckle on my sword.
("For surely I shall carry
Till the two of us part
In death the image
Of David in my heart.)

"As I would smite, even
Farther than the spear,
Here is my bow, David,
For thee to bear.

("For surely who shall rive it
When it beats no more
Shall find David's image
At my heart's core.)

"As I love thee, even,
I strip me of my girdle,
The royal symbol, David,
To bind about thy middle,
    David,
To bind about thy middle!"

And the lark sang to Jonathan
Lovely and loud,
The lark sang to Jonathan,
The lark in the cloud.

48

THE CROWS AT THE PARTING OF DAVID AND JONATHAN

Above the stone of Ezel
Querulous and high
Through the broken morning
Did the caw-crows cry.

They alone had witnessed
And the eye of the sun,
The banishment of David
From the sight of Jonathan.

Jonathan, shooting
While his lad stood apart,
Loosed three arrows
(From his bow to his heart.)

Loosed three arrows
Eastward at the sun,
And when his lad sought them
He cried: "They fell beyond!

("Past all finding
The arrows speed apart
That signal David's going
And the death of my heart.

"Past all knowing
The arrows have flown
That turn him to the wilderness
And my heart to stone.")

When the little lad, laden
With the bow had gone,
David came from hiding
By the great black stone.

And they two in silence
While the shadows at tether
Followed forth the sun
Sat bleeding together.

As each to each aching
Their slashed wrists bled
Jonathan, caressing
The palm of David, said:

"As I was dreaming, David,
Dreaming of thee,
Fair and kind, David,
You came to me.

"Against my heart, David,
I dreamed you leaned to rest,
But I might not embrace thee
And honor my breast.

"Your fevered fingers, David,
Burned mine like a brand,
But I might not caress thee
And honor my hand.

"Your lips were sweeter, David,
Than dew where honey drips,
But I might never kiss thee
And honor my lips, David,
And honor my lips.

"But now thou art banished
From the house of Saul
And I shall not encounter
Thee daily in his hall,
"Nor press with thee to battle,
Nor listen to thy lyre,
I lean to thee to kindle
My heart to fire.

"Since henceforth thou art banished
Forever from my sight,
(See the sun falling
Westward into night,)

"And I no more may wait thee
Whatever place I stand,
I take thy own to handsel
Love's fury in my hand.

"And yet, now thou art banished
By Saul from Israel -
Until the time fulfilling
The dreams of Samuel

"When the seeming endless
Way thou must set upon,
Proud path that in the turning
Shall lead to Israel's throne,

"Brings thee again to Gibeah,
I lean to kiss thy chaste
Lips brushed with salt of sorrow
And death's dear honey taste.

"Now may the Lord forever
Keep watch between us two."
So Jonathan and David
Said adieu.

When David's form retreating
Was little on the plain
And Jonathan had turned him
Homeward once again,

Above the stone of Ezel,
Querulous and high
In the broken evening
The crows began to cry:

"Jonathan, Jonathan
The son of Saul
Turns about from Ezel
To seek the end of all.

"Turns his face from Ezel,
Does the son of the king,
Looking toward Gilboa
As if it were the ring

"Set with the seal
And signet of his race,
Turns about from Ezel
His death-devoted face,

"Turns about from Ezel,
From David, all alone
And looks toward Gilboa
As if it were his throne.

"Jonathan, Jonathan
The fair son of Saul
Hastens forth to Bethshan
To hang upon the wall,

"Saying: *Did David
But trample with his feet
My bare bones bleaching
My death were sweet;*

"*And his hot hand about them
Shall be close as my flesh
As weeping he buries them
In the sepulchre of Kish!*"

THE COUNTRY HOUSEWIFE TELLS A ROSARY

The country housewife tells a rosary
Of browning beans and crimson peppers hung
From joist and ceiling; in her pantry she
Has stored for winter treats to tempt the tongue.
And safe in cellar, spilling from the bin,
Are apples stored to mellow in the dark
And bring up tasting sweet and earthy when
The apple tree stands winter-bare and stark.

Her husband's axe rings in the autumn wood
Felling the oaken tree to make a blaze
For winter evenings, as warm and good
Against the flesh as sun in summer days.
And comforted and warm these two shall lie
While northers whistle and the drifts pile high.

MANKIN'S SONG

Under the elm tree, under the cherry,
Under the oak tree in the glen,
I have been miserable and merry,
And merry and miserable again.

Beneath the rooftree, beneath the rafter,
Beneath the wide arch of the years
My tears have all rippled into laughter,
My laughter has taggled into tears.

I have given one coin to pay the piper,
I have piped one tune for the selfsame fee;
The corn I carried to the hopper
Returned as meal again to me.

And even-steven's a bargain surely;
Each winter was given my good regard
If winter was hard when spring was early
And spring was early when winter hard.

UNDERGROUND

In that subterranean city
To which I came at last
A ghost walked, and was pity,
And the ghost walked past and past.
At the middle of the bells, at midnight,
Help! cried a bundle of bones.

In that tunnel under the surface
Of light a presence moved,
And that presence had a luminous face
That only the damned have loved.
At the middle bells, at midnight,
O help! cried a bundle of bones.

In that cavern strictly shapen,
Boxed into four-square cells,
A strange thing came to happen
At the sound of the middle bells.
O help! cried the bones at midnight;
Compassion and pity sealed
In that subterranean city
Came, and the bones were healed
At the middle bells, at midnight
In that city underground.

MY TRUE LOVE

Blacker than night is my True-Love's hair,
My True-Love's brow is bonny;
My True-Love's lips are ruby and fair
And touched with the taste of honey.

Whiter than milk is my True-Love's throat
That soars like a marble column
And bears a bell of marvelous note
With accents airy and solemn.

Tender and strong are my True-Love's hands,
Their strength by mercy made dearer;
Each five of fingers are fiercer than brands
And total a ten of terror.

Because it is dearer to breathe than breath
And low and more utter than loathing,
My love for my True-Love is darker than death
And whiter than Christ's own clothing.

I taste of the Wine from my True-Love's lips,
And bread is my True-Love's body;
And the vinegar waits at my fingertips,
And the Cross stands hewn and ready.

BALLAD OF THE RIDER

Under the little leaves of life
Helmer rode in a stranger's land,
Bearing beneath his coat a knife
Well fitted to his hand.

The little leaves were green and trim
And the wind was soft and kind,
But shy wild things took flight from
    him
With murder on his mind.

He left his house, he left his land,
He left his countryside,
With the knife well fitted to his hand,
To seek his wandered bride.

"Her laugh was free, her step was
    light,
Her eyes outflamed the dawn;
Her lips were wine of a strange
    delight,"
He mused as he rode on.

"Were she a lesser prize to win,
Or a wench a man would choose
To warm his boughten bed, why then
She were not so much to lose.

"But her love was like a burning bush
On a wide and darkling plain,
Or a voice continually saying *hush*
To whimperings of pain.

"If I have not her warmth by night
Nor her bright look by day
For body's need and soul's delight
I vow no other may.

"I'll search a thousand miles of ground
To be her murderer;
Or if she be by water bound
I'll search the seas for her."

So on he rode both night and day
By alien hill and tree,
Stopping at dwellings by the way
With words of inquiry.

"This lady of the search," said they
"How shall we know her as
The one you seek; how tell her, pray,
From other maids that pass?"

"Her laugh is free, her step is light,
Her eyes outflame the dawn,
Her lips are wine of a strange delight,"
He said and so rode on.

Beneath the solitudinous boughs
That shake on many a hill
Helmer bore his bitter vows
As an armor to his will.

He sat by many a family fire,
Nor warmth nor bread sought he
But sat thus only to inquire
His ceaseless inquiry.

"This lady, should she come,"
    said they,
"How shall we know her as
The one you seek; how know her,
    pray,
From any maid that pass?"

"She had a way of making light
And a way of making dread
As if a witch or water sprite
Had lodging in her head."

And so he rode till autumn flamed
With crimson shoemake fire;
And though her name was never
   named
He ceased not to inquire.
"This lady of the search," said they,
"How shall we know her as
The one you seek, if on a day
She chance this way to pass?"

"To cold she is the warming sun,
To desert thirst, a flood;
She is the cool of summer dawn,
And a fever in the blood."

Among the little rounded hills
That step up from the sea
He rested on the brown pine spills
To make his inquiry.

"A twelvemonth past she came,"
   they said,
"But she has journeyed on,
Singing upon a road that led
Into the gates of dawn."

"A six-month past she came,"
   they said,
"But vanished with the spring,
Sighing upon a road that led
To the halls of evening."

"A fortnight gone she came,"
   they said,
"Your lady of delight,
Crying most dismally, and sped
Into the windy night."

And when he questioned by the way
Where highland poplars wave:
"News of her death had we," said they,
but no one knows her grave."

Then Helmer rode most bitterly
Into a winter dawn;
"I've sought her through the earth,"
   said he,
"I'll seek her now beyond."
But whether wind blow north or west
Or whether east or south,
The knife he bore is in his breast,
The mould is on his mouth;

And what pale palfrey shall he ride,
What magic-metalled knife
Have power to harm his wandered
   bride
Beyond the leaves of life!

MOUNTAIN FIDDLER

I took my fiddle
That sings and cries
To a hill in the middle
Of Paradise.

I sat at the base
Of a golden stone
In that holy place
To play alone.

I tuned the strings
And began to play,
And a crowd of wings
Were bent my way.

A voice said
Amid the stir:
"We that were dead,
O Fiddler,

"With purest gold
Are robed and shod,
And we behold
The face of God.

"Our halls can show
No thing so rude
As your horsehair bow,
Or your fiddlewood;

"And yet can they
So well entrance
If you but play
Then we must dance!"

THE ADORATION

If I but had a little dress,
A little dress of the flax so fair
I'd take it from my clothespress
And give it to Him to wear,
    To wear,
And give to Him to wear.

If I but had a little girdle
A girdle stained with the purple dye,
Or green as grass or green as myrtle
About His waist to tie,
    To tie,
About His waist to tie!

If I but had a little coat,
A coat to fit a no-year-old,
I'd button it close about His throat
To cover Him from the cold,
    The cold,
To cover Him from the cold.

If I but had a little shoe,
A little shoe as might be found
I'd lace it on with a sheepskin thew
To keep His foot from the ground,
    The ground,
To keep His foot from the ground.

If my heart were a shining coin,
A silver coin or a coin of gold
Out of my side I'd it purloin
And give it to Him to hold,
    To hold,
And give it to Him to hold.

If my heart were a house also,
A house also with room to spare
I never would suffer my Lord to go
Homeless, but house Him there,
    O there,
Homeless, but house Him there.

ROADS

A pace or two beyond my door
Are highways racing east and west,
I hear their busy traffic roar,
Fleet tourists bound on far behests
And monstrous mastodons of freight
Passing in droves before my gate.
The roads would tow me far away
To cities whose extended pull
They have no choice but to convey;
I name them great and wonderful
And marvels of device and speed,
But all unsuited to my need.

My heart is native to the sky
Where hills that are its only wall
Stand up to judge its boundaries by;
But where from roofs of iron fall
Sheer perpendiculars of steel
On streets that bruise the country heel

My heart's contracted to a stone.
Therefore whatever roads repair
To cities on the plain, my own
Lead upward to the peaks; and there
I feel, pushing my ribs apart
The wide sky entering my heart.

THE GIFTING

There was a giving once of gifts,
And that was done in Bethlehem;
The Magi gifted Mary there
And Mary gifted them.

The three were men of much account,
Each was a king in his own country;
Mary she was a poor lady
And meek and mild was she.

The three came bearing costly gifts,
Each from his treasury could choose;
Mary gave the greatest gift
Of all, no matter whose.

The Wise Men gave three gifts, all told,
Three gifts to Mary's one,
Myrrh and frankincense and gold-
But Mary, Christ her Son!

A BOY'S WEATHER

I KNOW how is seems within a boy's head,
Having myself been young not long ago,
Nothing is finer, after all is said,
Weather has power to offer than a snow.
A shower may prove a respite from the field
But only briefly, and it clogs his feet
When he returns, it is a drudge concealed;
Only a snow is perfect and complete.

No sooner than November's lease is secure
And the first snowflakes are a prophecy,
Than he must rise at night and see for sure
Whether they mean to speak the truth or lie;
Seeing white proof the flakes meant what they said
He shuts the shutters and goes back to bed.

GATHERS AGAIN TO SHINING

I am that creature born to eat the dust
The alchemists of bole and leaf transmute
From solvent soil in which the root is thrust
Into the gold and wonder-shapen fruit.
When windy trumpets signal winter weather,
Impelled by such a need as prompts the squirrel
To hoard the hickory nut, I go and gather
A dusty harvest into bin and barrel.

Yet I am he who feasts upon a star;
I taste the sun when eating of the fruit
Shaped in the image of that globe afar
From whence the leaves brought down their heavenly loot
Of light that once unlocked from apple and grain
Gathers again to shining in my brain.

A SONG OF SORROW

O MEN, come in from the field and lane
And pray over Sarah's one daughter again
For she is possessed of a terrible pain.

O men, come in and softly abide
In reverent silence with your knees spread wide
For Sarah's one daughter has suffered and died.

O men, come in from the field and plow
And pick at your teeth with the tip of a bough,
And say to her kindly brave words for tomorrow
For Sarah's possessed of a pitiful sorrow.

PRODIGAL

II
Yea, I shall turn again to my own land
When breath is miser-meted, and the low
Voice that spoke in youth and bade me go
Fails in the tongues it had on every hand.
I shall return, I shall go home again
To native hills and valleys, where of these
The brooks ventriloquize, and every breeze
Speaks of familiars of hill and plain.

And there when Fall has vagaried the bee
And wrecked the spider's house and sent the bird
To seek the shelter of a southern tree,
No longer willing to be held or stirred
The leaves of life that stem from heart and brow
May join their brothers flying from the bough.

I KNOW A VALLEY GREEN WITH CORN

I know a valley green with corn
Where Nottley's waters roil and run
From the deep hills where first at morn
It takes the color of the sun

And bears it burning through the shade
Of birch and willow till its tide
Pours like a pulse, and never stayed,
Dark where the Gulf's edge reaches wide.

There, while the twilight spends its dream
Of light and shadow both, the whir
Of bats and cry of doves will seem
A very liveness of the air

About a house the ivy's foot
Creeps slowly up to hide the eaves
And wreathe the chimney, dark with soot,
Into a colonnade of leaves.

And one will loiter in the yard
Soft shadowed by the last of day
As if she waited for a word
From lips three thousand miles away

That yearn to speak against her hair
But, dumb behind the palm of space
Tauten to trembling, while there
Darkness obliterates her face.

Suggestions for Further Reading

BYRON HERBERT REECE'S six books were originally published by E.P. Dutton in New York. The four volumes of poetry are *Ballad of the Bones and Other Poems* (1945), *Bow Down in Jericho* (1950). *The Season of Flesh* (1955), and *A Song of Joy and Other Poems* (1952). The novels are *Better a Dinner of Herbs* (1950) and *The Hawk and the Sun* (1955). All six titles were reprinted in 1985 by Cherokee Publishing Company, a division of the Larlin Corporation of Marietta, Georgia.

Mountain Singer: The Life and Legacy of Byron Herbert Reece, by Raymond A. Cook, reprinted by Cherokee Publishing Company in 1985, is the only comprehensive biography of Reece and contains, in addition, 167 pages of selected poems and a thorough bibliography of news stories and articles about the poet. *The Georgia Review*, volume XII, number 4 (Winter, 1958) contains commemorative essays by Jesse Stuart, Elizabeth Stevenson, Mildred White Greear, and Ralph McGill.

Manuscript and other material relating to the poet are in the Duckworth Library, Young Harris College; The Byron Herbert Reece Collection, Hargrett Rare Book Manuscript Library, University of Georgia; and the Special Collections Library of Emory University.

Index of Poems

Acknowledgements

THE PHOTOGRAPHS of Reece on pages v, 4, 12, the covers, and the frontispiece are courtesy of *The Atlanta Journal and Constitution*. The photographs on pages 17, 18, and 28 are reprinted with the kind permission of the Byron Herbert Reece Collection, Hargrett Rare Book and Manuscript Library, University of Georgia.

"The Tree, the Bird, and the Leaf" appeared in the *New Orleans Poetry Journal* of April, 1955, and is quoted here with kind permission of the Byron Herbert Reece Collection, Hargrett Rare Book and Manuscript Library, University of Georgia. "Ballad of the Weaver," "Bitter Berry," "A Boy's Weather," "Elbows on the Sky," "I Go By Way of Rust and Flame," "Invocation," "Lest the Lonesome Bird," "Mountain Fiddler," "A Song of Sorrow," and "Whose Eye is on the Sparrow" were published in *Ballad of the Bones and Other Poems* (New York: E.P. Dutton, 1950; Atlanta, Georgia: Cherokee Press, 1985); "The Adoration," "As I Lie Down," "The Country Housewife Tells a Rosary," "The Crows at the Parting of David and Jonathan," "Gathers Again to Shining," "The Larks at the Meeting of David and Jonathan," "Now That Spring is Here," "Prodigal II," "Roads," "The Speechless Kingdom," "Three Times Already I Have Outwitted Death," and "We Could Wish Them a Longer Stay" appeared in *Bow Down in Jericho* (New York: E.P. Dutton, 1950; Atlanta, Georgia: Cherokee Press, 1985); "A Song of Joy," "From Chips and Shards," "I Know a Valley Green With Corn," "Mankin's Song," "O Elements," "The Sound of Rain," and "There Never Was Time" are from *A Song of Joy and Other Poems* (New York: E.P. Dutton, 1952; Atlanta, Georgia: Cherokee Press, 1985); "The Gifting," "The Haying," "In Absence," "In the Corridor," "My True Love," "The Stay-at-Home," and "Underground," are from *The Season of Flesh* (New York: E.P. Dutton, 1955; Atlanta, Georgia: Cherokee Press, 1985). These poems are quoted with kind permission of Cherokee Press.

About the Author

BETTIE SELLERS is a poet and teacher. She is Goolsby Professor of English at Young Harris College, where she has been a member of the faculty since 1965. Her published volumes of poetry include *Wild Ginger* (1989), *Liza's Monday and Other Poems* (1986), and *Morning of the Red-Tailed Hawk* (1986). She is the author of several articles on Byron Herbert Reece and writer and co-producer of the documentary video, "The Bitter Berry: The Life and Work of Byron Herbert Reece."